IMAGES
of America

CAMP EDWARDS AND OTIS AIR FORCE BASE

The Massachusetts Military Reservation has had its dramatic moments in connection with combat units formed and trained on site for the national military services, but it has long been the working home of Massachusetts soldiers. Here the Headquarters and Service Troop of the Quincy Armory poses for a picture at Camp Edwards during a summer drill in 1946. In the third row, third from the left, stands Pvt. Frederick E. Morin of Quincy. (Morin.)

ON THE COVER: The Antiaircraft Artillery Training Center's obstacle course at Camp Edwards prepared hundreds of men for combat in World War II. (FSA.)

IMAGES
of America

CAMP EDWARDS AND
OTIS AIR FORCE BASE

Donald J. Cann and John J. Galluzzo

ARCADIA
PUBLISHING

Copyright © 2010 by Donald J. Cann and John J. Galluzzo
ISBN 978-0-7385-7214-7

Published by Arcadia Publishing
Charleston SC, Chicago IL, Portsmouth NH, San Francisco CA

Printed in the United States of America

Library of Congress Control Number: 2009929403

For all general information contact Arcadia Publishing at:
Telephone 843-853-2070
Fax 843-853-0044
E-mail sales@arcadiapublishing.com
For customer service and orders:
Toll-Free 1-888-313-2665

Visit us on the Internet at www.arcadiapublishing.com

*Dedicated to all of the men and women who served and continue
to serve at the various military installations of Camp Edwards and
the Otis airbase. We thank you for your service to our country.*

CONTENTS

ACKNOWLEDGMENTS

The authors would like to thank the numerous individuals and organizations who made the production of this book possible: Ian Meisner, former executive director of the Fort Devens Museum, and Kara Fossey, his successor, both of whom were instrumental in the telling of the German mock village story; Capt. John B. Shealy, Massachusetts Army National Guard Training Site, Massachusetts Military Reservation, for a guided tour of the grounds; Dr. Susan Goodfellow, Environmental and Readiness Center, cultural resource manager, Massachusetts Military Reservation, Camp Edwards; Lynda E. Wadsworth, public outreach manager, Environmental and Readiness Center, Massachusetts National Guard, Massachusetts Military Reservation, Camp Edwards; M.Sgt. Katherine Perez, National Guard Bureau Public Affairs; Jeff Buczkowki, lieutenant colonel, U.S. Army Public Affairs; Brig. Gen. Leonid Kondratiuk, director, Historical Services, the Commonwealth of Massachusetts, Military Division, Office of the Adjutant General; Col. Anthony "KIMO" Schiavi, 102nd Intelligence Wing, commander; Lt. Col. Christopher M. Faux, Mission Support Group commander, 102nd Intelligence Wing; Evan C. Lagasse, civilian, Massachusetts Air National Guard, 102nd Intelligence Wing public affairs specialist; Timothy Muldoon, part-time curator, Massachusetts Air National Guard Historical Association; Joan Gearin, National Archives and Records Administration, Waltham, Massachusetts; Fred Morin, Massachusetts Aviation Historical Society historian; Capt. Nicole Ivers, Public Affairs, 102nd Intelligence Wing; Janet Cann; Michelle Galluzzo; and the staff of the National Archives and Records Administration II Building in College Park, Maryland.

Photograph abbreviations are as follows: ACE is the Army Corps of Engineers; FDM is the Fort Devens Museum; FSA is the Farming Security Administration; MANG is the Massachusetts Air National Guard; MANGHA is the Massachusetts Air National Guard Historical Association; MNG is the Massachusetts National Guard; Morin is Fred Morin; and NARA is the National Archives and Records Administration.

INTRODUCTION

The need for a formalized military came early in Massachusetts history. Although each settlement had its military-style leaders, for instance Myles Standish in the Plymouth settlement, standing armies were by no means the ordinary state of affairs. On December 13, 1636, the Massachusetts Bay Colonial Militia formed, the ancient antecedent of today's Massachusetts National Guard. Through skirmishes and wars with local Native American tribes, the American Revolution, the War of 1812, the Civil War, and the Spanish-American War, not to mention other minor conflicts, the men of Massachusetts trained and fought for freedom and democracy. It took three centuries for the Massachusetts National Guard to find a permanent home.

The wilds of Cape Cod beckoned to Massachusetts's soldiers as early as 1908. Weekend and summer training among the pitch pines took place south and west of what would become the Massachusetts Military Reservation. Shortly after, in 1917, Camp Devens in Central Massachusetts was formed to ready troops for combat in World War I and in 1931 was designated a permanent installation for the state's militia. Even then, though, the state's military leaders knew it was not sufficient for all of the training that would be needed. That year, a board of six Army National Guard officers were tasked with finding a site big enough to accommodate all of the phases of training Massachusetts soldiers would go through, particularly paying attention to the ever-increasing ranges of new forms of artillery. Two years later, the board of six returned a report stating that the open land needed existed in the unsettled wilderness of the Upper Cape. In 1935, Gov. James Michael Curley signed a bill for the appropriation of funds to purchase the needed lands, and the following year, the first troops took to the field. The plans for the base included the laying out of two turf runways to provide for training in military aviation. So were born Camp Edward and Otis Field, the main components of the Massachusetts Military Reservation.

The timing proved to be fortuitous for the American military. With storm clouds brewing over Europe, the possibility of the United States ending its long era of isolationism seemed great. The 26th "Yankee" Division of the Massachusetts National Guard headed south for training in the fall of 1941, returning to Camp Edwards on December 6. The following day, the Japanese attack on Pearl Harbor ensured American participation in what would become World War II. Cape Cod would become a massive training and testing ground for the military, from Aqua Cheetahs at Sandy Neck, to DUKWs at Provincetown, from amphibian landings across the sound on Martha's Vineyard, to night antiaircraft artillery firings at Wellfleet.

World War II was the heyday of Camp Edwards, as the acquired space filled up quickly to accommodate convalescent hospitals, seasickness research, a German prisoner of war (POW) camp, firing ranges of all types, and the ever-expanding runways of Otis Field.

The end of the war brought a silence to the area that had not been heard in five years, as America's surviving military men mustered out of service. Nearly 13,000 men were discharged from the service at Camp Edwards in 1945 and 1946. Deactivated from federal service in 1946, the Massachusetts Military Reservation was returned to the use of the state's troops, who continued to train there. The Army Air Corps became the U.S. Air Force, which quickly established ties to Air National Guard units. Propeller planes gave way to jets, and the hot firing of weapons in training prepared troops for a cold war. Allies in World War II became paper enemies as an American president learned to call the base his working home near his summer home.

It would be impossible to tell the story of every unit that served at the Massachusetts Military Reservation in the pages of this book. Many units moved through quickly, especially during World War II, and the various changes that took place—names changes, mission changes, and so on—provide a tangled web that is just not fun reading for a superficial history of such a deeply historical place. The authors have attempted to relate the basics of the Edwards and Otis stories, to describe everyday life on base and to provide a snapshot in time, mostly of World War II on the reservation. We have not referred in great detail to training accidents that resulted in deaths, nor have we considered discussing the recent cleanup issues. That topic is better handled by folks closer to the story.

On tours of the base in 2008, the authors were privileged to see the remaining buildings still standing from the World War II era and to see firsthand the training sites now in use on the base. We were surprised, but pleased, as historians, to tour a mock Middle Eastern village prepared for urban combat training. The site mirrored the construction of a German village built at Camp Edwards during World War II. We witnessed the construction of a replica base end station, like those being used by our troops in Afghanistan and Iraq, and met the men and women of the Massachusetts National Guard and the 102nd Intelligence Wing.

On September 11, 2001, F-15 Eagles, from what was then the 102nd Fighter Wing, were the first American military planes to respond to the terrorist attacks on the World Trade Center in New York City. They responded from the airfield that now stands on what, in 1935, was simply two flattened stretches of turf named for a flight surgeon lost on a training mission. While downsizing has been a military buzzword for years, history has shown that Americans will always have to be prepared to expect the unexpected, and that the flexibility of a place like the Massachusetts Military Reservation will continue to make it valuable to the Massachusetts and American militaries for years to come.

One

BUILDING THE MASSACHUSETTS MILITARY RESERVATION

With World War I already well underway in Europe, the United States began preparations to join the conflict in 1917. Calling upon the strength of the state national guards, the American military began training for what would be bloody, deadly combat. Warfare technologies had outraced strategic tactical thinking, meaning that waves of men were running into volleys of guns firing more rounds faster than ever before. Training properly could simply save a man's life, and it would be the hallmark of Camp Edwards from the 1930s into the 21st century. (NARA.)

While designating and naming a site for a military reservation may have been a relatively simple task, when one considers the site requirements, most prominently, the needed acreage, designing and building that base was a much more difficult job. With maps hung on the wall to their backs, more stored in bins to their left, and rudimentarily hung electric lights dangling above their makeshift desks, engineers and architects sketched plans that eventually led to the construction of the home to nearly 100,000 military men at different times during World War II, the Massachusetts Military Reservation. (MANGHA.)

The site would need to house troops by the thousands. It would need training grounds of varied types, some for weapons not even thought of yet. It would need hospitals, churches, and recreation facilities. It would need airfields for the burgeoning field of military aviation. It would need to be a place that would serve the military's training purposes while maintaining the morale of the men that military would need to carry out its missions. By 1938, Massachusetts's military men were camping on cleared lands in anticipation of the construction of "permanent" wooden barracks. By March 1941, thirty-thousand soldiers had filled the cantonments of Camp Edwards and begun training for what many expected to be America's entry into the second global war in just over two decades. (MANGHA.)

The building behind the two men on guard duty is a typical World War II barrack of the 700 series of cantonment (temporary quarters). Camp Edwards was the first site where this series of cantonments were built. As a result of the success of this construction, the 700 series was built across the country. In January 1941, the U.S. Army could provide housing for 315,000 troops. By January 1943, housing was available for 4.6 million. (MNG.)

The plan called for a 1,722-bed hospital. Carpenters are working on the roof of the hospital administration building in this photograph. This hospital staff of pioneers was one of the first responsible for finding a way to prevent seasickness and in treating wounded soldiers coming back from the war in Europe and the Pacific. (MNG.)

This location is known as the South Truck Road. Initial construction took place between 1936 and 1940. The Works Progress Administration (WPA) provided funds to construct 63 buildings and two turf runways, which were named Otis Field after 1st Lt. Frank J. Otis. This was the biggest WPA project in the state. (MNG.)

In this photograph, the buildings are up and the electrical wires have been strung, but the grounds are unfinished. September 14, 1940, Congress enacted the first peacetime draft. Two days later, Pres. Franklin D. Roosevelt signed the Selective Training and Service Act. With the need to house the men taken into the armed forces, the U.S. Army leased Camp Edwards for 99 years in 1940. That year, they started building quarters to accommodate 30,000 troops. This project was completed in 125 days. (MNG.)

This is the South Outer Road, and in this photograph, finish work is still being done before the buildings are occupied. The U.S. Department of Defense and the National Park Service published a history of the 700 and 800 series cantonment construction, and Camp Edwards was featured in the history, as it became a prototype for future temporary quarters all over the United States. (MNG.)

The barracks were designed to hold 63 men apiece. Maj. Thomas Waters was the first camp commander. It was during his time in command that the major part of the construction was completed. The general contractor was the Walsh Construction Company of Davenport, Iowa. However, as much as possible, subcontractors were local. These included Charles Main, architect engineering; Crystal Concrete Company of Braintree; and F. V. Laurence Plant of Falmouth, concrete. (MNG.)

In this photograph of one- and two-story buildings, there are still some of the scrub pines from the forest that was removed for the construction. In later photographs, even the trees that had survived the construction seemed to have vanished. (MNG.)

This photograph of barracks all in a row also shows an open place that will become a truck park. Buildings in this project, according to the government report, include "438 barracks, 184 mess halls, 54 officers' quarters and mess building, 31 administrative buildings, 28 storage buildings, 13 chapels, 217 recreation structures, 82 hospital units and 314 miscellaneous structures." (MNG.)

Smaller structures served as company headquarters, dayrooms, supply rooms, and arms repair shops, and company and officers' mess halls. In addition, there were libraries and service clubs and other buildings that had functions within the cantonment area. (MNG.)

A 4-mile railroad spur was built from the North Falmouth station. This photograph was taken shortly after the spur was built. The track bed and the bridges all were constructed to enable trains to get to Camp Edwards. Construction material was delivered by rail instead of by the 11 miles of road from the closest rail yard. Later coal to heat the buildings was delivered along the same tracks. Troops' trains arrived and departed, including the special convalescent trains of wounded soldiers. (MNG.)

This is one of the various small frame buildings in the cantonment areas being constructed. A mass production system was used to construct the camp buildings. Fifteen-man crews performed one task, such as foundations; the next crew framed the first-floor decks; and the next would frame the walls on the ground of a one-story building and raised them complete with their sheathing. (MNG.)

The Architect Engineers Report of Charles T. Main, Inc., of June 4, 1941, reported that "the main cantonment area had been organized under the First Army as a standard National Guard square with a total of twenty regiments blocks for infantry and artillery regiments." The new main camp was laid out around the existing quadrangle. Inside the regimental square, three regimental groups were located to each side of a 1-mile-square parade ground. The general pattern of the individual regimental layout was as follows: on the edges of the parade ground was located the regimental administration buildings, officers' quarters, and mess halls. Between the inner roads (around the parade grounds) and the outer road were located the company storehouses and miscellaneous regimental buildings, including the guard house, infirmary, exchanges, dayrooms, and company mess halls. Beyond the outer road are barracks, storehouses, motor repair shops, gasoline stations, truck parks, and so on. Outside the main cantonment, additional blocks were constructed for the hospital, logistics, quartermaster, "colored" infantry, and service commands. (MNG.)

The cantonments were finished in December 1940. A payroll of almost $1 million a week was paid to 18,593 workers at the peak of construction. The designers, engineers, buildings tradesmen, and the army all learned skills that were used across the country in the building of barracks for the troops who fought in World War II. The first troops that occupied these particular buildings arrived December 18, 1940. They were two units that had been tenting for four months, the 68th and the 198th Coast Artillery Regiments. The Yankee Division arrived in January 1941. As units were transferred, other units replaced them. Some of the units that were assigned to Camp Edwards were the 26th Infantry Division and the 182nd Infantry Regiment, the 101st Observation Squadron, the 14th Antisubmarine Patrol Squadron, the Second Battalion, 64th Coastal Artillery, and the Army Engineer Amphibian Command. Here Pvt. Philip Halpern of Company K, 104th Infantry, is checking his equipment after returning from southern maneuvers, September 6, 1941. He was one of 30,000 troops stationed at Camp Edwards that year; in comparison, the Cape Cod civilian population at that time was 37,295. (NARA.)

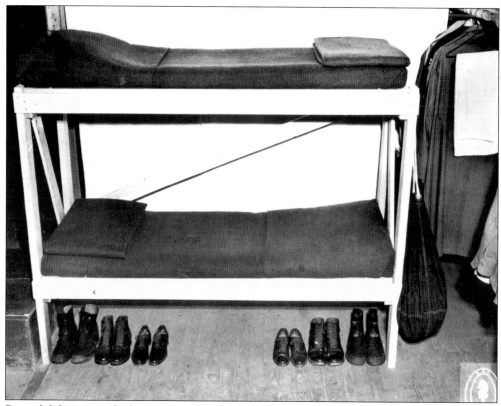

Barrack life was much the same for all soldiers, with two-man bunks and a prescribed way of caring for and displaying equipment and personal items. This photograph and the three that follow were used by Camp Edwards commanders to set standards for personal space and locker inspections. (NARA.)

This photograph gives a better view of the display of a soldier's web gear for inspection. It also shows the lineup of shoes and footlockers. (NARA.)

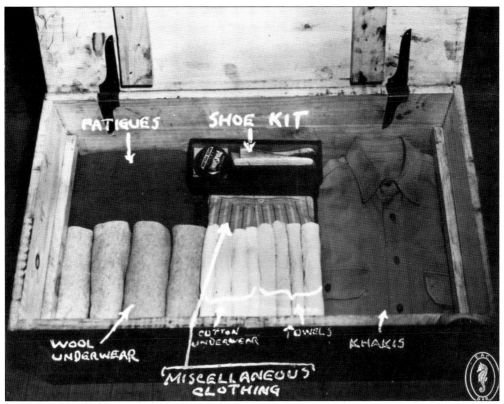

FATIGUES   SHOE KIT

WOOL
UNDERWEAR

COTTON
UNDERWEAR   TOWELS   KHAKIS

MISCELLANEOUS
CLOTHING

This is the required inspection display of personal items in an army footlocker within the barracks. Often soldiers had two sets of the items seen here, one set for inspection and one or more sets to use. (NARA.)

This is the removable tray of the footlocker. Inspections were one of the things that made life in the barracks unlike living at home. (NARA.)

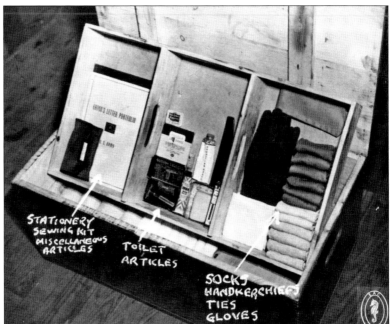

STATIONERY
SEWING KIT
MISCELLANEOUS
ARTICLES

TOILET
ARTICLES

SOCKS
HANDKERCHIEFS
TIES
GLOVES

Life at Camp Edwards was a mixture of pleasure and work. This is M.Sgt. Clayton Mitchell of the Engineer Amphibian Command, preparing for one of his regular radio broadcasts in one of the 13 chapels built on Camp Edwards. Thousands of men would pass through the gates to the camp during World War II, and some would never return to their homes. For those men and women that survived the war, memories of life at Camp Edwards would be woven into the larger fabric of the experience of a country at war. (NARA.)

Two

CAMP LIFE

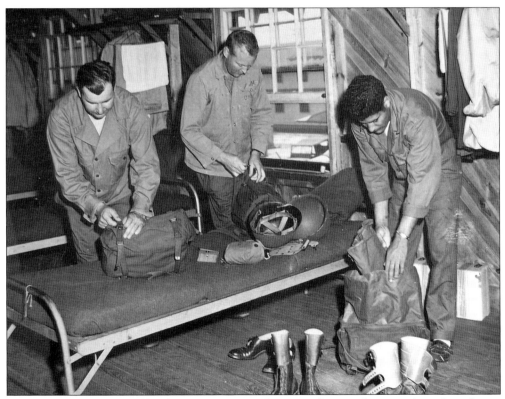

"Hurry up and wait," the old military saying goes. There was plenty to do on a military base during wartime, but the "brass" knew that even the best of fighting men could crack without a proper amount of rest and recreation to balance out the hectic training schedule. While these men were packing their gear for bivouac on July 10, 1950, they knew that a cold beer and a song on a jukebox were not that far away. Military life was not all drilling and formations. (NARA.)

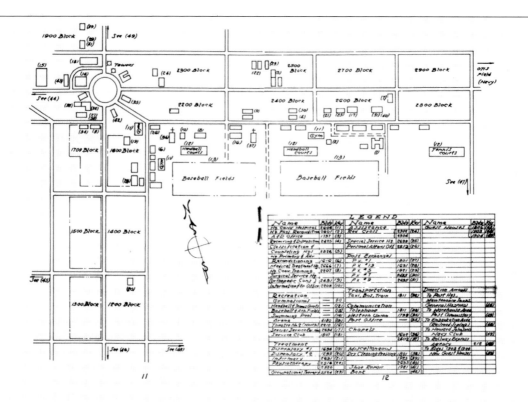

This plan shows the organization of the troop quarters in the 1940s; the block-and-grid system is used. Roads, buildings, and athletic fields were named for Massachusetts National Guardsmen who served in World War I and were deceased at the time of the new construction. Fredrickson Road was named for 1st Lt. Gunnar Fredrickson, 110th Cavalry. Estey Road was named for Major Harold Watson Estey, 101st Engineers. Guenther Road was named for Pvt. Charles Richard Guenther, 101st Infantry. The hospital was named for Col. Frank P. William, commanding officer of the 101st Medical Regiment. The plan shows two baseball fields and important activities for free time. The baseball field in the 101st Field Artillery area was named Dewart Field for 1st Lt. Murray W. Dewart, chaplain of this unit in World War I. (MNG.)

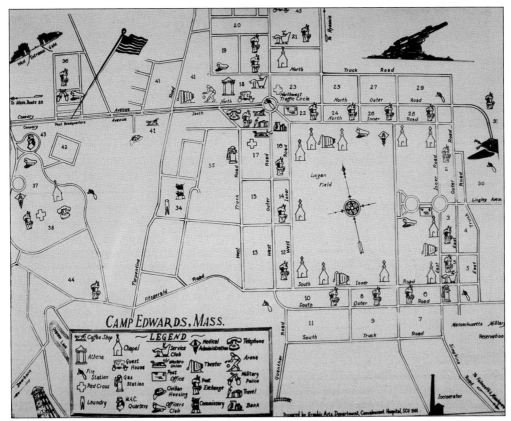

CAMP EDWARDS, MASS.

~LEGEND~

Coffee Shop | Service Club | Medical Administration | Telephone
Athena | Chapel | Western Union | Arena
Fire Station | Guest House | Theater | Military Police
Red Cross | Gas Station | Post Office | Travel
Laundry | Civilian Housing | Post Exchange |
W.A.C. Quarters | Officers Club | Commissary | Bank

Prepared by Graphic Arts Department, Convalescent Hospital, SCU 1182.

Richard Bennett Talcott wrote a booklet called *Camp Edwards* in 1942 describing his experiences while stationed there. He lists the recreational opportunities on base: service clubs, movie theaters, an amphitheater for stage shows, a sports arena, a fine beach, ball courts, and several baseball fields. (NARA.)

Talcott mentioned Old Silver Beach, on Nantucket Sound, as a beach for the "well to-do." He described it as a white-sand beach on the warm side of the Cape, which "goes off gradually." This was the beach the soldiers were able to use. This photograph shows the workaday side of a beach, with amphibian engineers and infantry practicing beach landings on Sandy Neck in 1942. (NARA.)

This is the rear of the 1941 headquarters of the 26th Yankee Division. Other units that used it as a headquarters were the 56th Antiaircraft Artillery Brigade and the 551st Airborne Early Warning and Control Wing. The gathering of civilians and soldiers is unidentified; there were many times when this type of gathering might take place, such as a change of command or the deployment of a unit. Note the searchlight in the photograph. (MNG.)

26

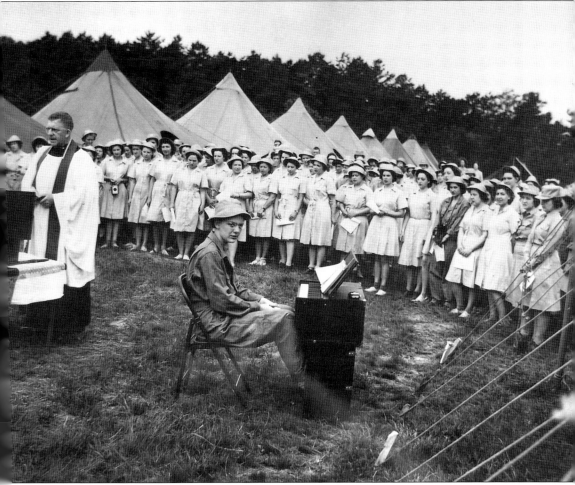

The Women's Auxiliary Arms Corps (WAAC) came to Camp Edwards in the spring of 1943. Their training was much like that of the male soldiers. They lived in a tent city for a week in the Mashpee woods, even though they worked in the hospital or in offices on base. After their training on the Cape, they went to serve in all the theaters of the war. In spite of having 13 chapels on base, the women here are having their service in the field. (NARA.)

This photograph dates from 1951 and is labeled "consolidated mess facility." The original mess halls were for a company. The officers' mess was designed for 118 people, and the enlisted men's was for 170. This mess hall has been modified to serve more than the original design. (MNG.)

Consolidated Mess
Facilities
Camp Edwards June 1951

This is the kitchen of the 1951 consolidated mess facility. (MNG.)

Feeding 30,000 men during World War II required apt logistics and storage facilities. This photograph is of meat in the cold storage. (MNG.)

Master Sergeant Salvaggio of Houston, Texas, holds a turkey in the base warehouse, which will be served at the base's Thanksgiving dinner on November 17, 1950. Bushel baskets filled with vegetables will add to the feast. (NARA.)

Joe Louis Barrow (the "Brown Bomber") was the heavyweight boxing champion from 1937 to 1949. Louis fought two charity bouts in 1942. The first, on January 9, was for the Navy Relief Society, where he defeated Buddy Baer. The amount of $47,000 was raised for the society. The next day, Louis enlisted in the army. March 23, 1942, he fought another charity bout against Abe Simon and raised $36,000 for the Army Relief Fund. In the army, he spent most of the time traveling from post to post in the United States and Europe, putting on a grand total of 96 exhibition bouts. He also is known for a recruiting poster with the quote, "We're going to do our part . . . and we'll win because we're on God's Side." On August 30, 1943, Louis put on an exhibition at Fort Devens and Camp Edwards, fighting with 1st Sgt. George Nicholson at Edwards. The September 13, 1943, issue of *Life* magazine had a photograph of the two and eight photographs of the Fort Devens demonstration. In this photograph, Louis is signing autographs at Camp Edwards. The soldiers are wearing the shoulder-sleeve insignia of the Department of the Army Staff Support. Louis's rank in this picture is a three-stripe sergeant. He achieved the rank of technical sergeant first class before his honorable discharge in 1945. He also was awarded the Legion of Merit. (MNG.)

One of the few World War II buildings that has survived into the 21st century is the sports arena. The second building along Connery Avenue is the arena. This building seats 4,000. Wrestling and, of course, boxing bouts drew large crowds, especially if the man in the ring was Joe Louis Barrow. Four basketball courts, a tennis court, and an indoor roller skating rink were a few of the recreation opportunities waiting for the GIs in the sports arena. This building was also used for United Service Organization (USO) events and dances. (NARA.)

This is the main hall of the service club. On the main floor was where the dances were held, as well as other activities. The gallery that wrapped around the interior offered a place to watch the dancers and a place to find an out of the way place to read or meet a friend. Amateur shows by soldiers, sing-alongs, ping-pong tournaments, checker games, and of course, a jukebox, were just some of the diversions from army life the service club offered. (MNG.)

The service club had a staff, which was hired by the U.S. Special Services. A special service officer who was in charge of the service club personnel ran the club. Staff consisted of himself, a senior hostess, and two junior hostesses. The staff often set up off-base excursions and could help a soldier who wanted to visit Boston or other places in New England. (MNG.)

The service club maintained a library on its second floor with over 5,000 volumes of general interest, as well as technical, books. There was also a mobile library that loaned books to soldiers. This service was provided by the State Department of Education. All one had to do was send a card with the title of the book, and it was delivered to the solider. (MNG.)

There were four movie theaters at Camp Edwards during World War II. They were built by the War Department and showed first-run movies. At times, a theater would stage a Broadway show or a radio broadcast, and at times, stage and screen stars would perform in one of the camp theaters. (MNG.)

This is the 35-mm film projector that was installed in one of the movie theaters. Some of the films that were hits in the 1940s were *The Great Dictator* (1940), *Sergeant York* (1941), *To Be or Not to Be* (1942), *Casablanca* (1942), and *For Whom the Bell Tolls* (1943), to name a few. (MNG.)

This is a view of the hospital as it looked on December 15, 1951. This base hospital dealt with the emergencies and sickness that would be expected where 30,000 soldiers were training for war. As the war progressed, many of the wounded were being sent home. The main specialty of this hospital was convalescence. Wounded soldiers came by the thousands. Those from the Northeast remained at the Camp Edwards Hospital, while those from other parts of the country were sent to hospitals near their home, as well as those who required specialized care, on special hospital trains. (NARA.)

This is an interior of one of the specially built and air-conditioned railroad ward cars used for the transporting of wounded soldiers from Camp Edwards to other hospitals. Maj. Arthur Coyne—commander of 114th Hospital Detachment and commanding officer of the Hospital Train Detachment—and nurses Doris Kennedy and Louise Brown are inspecting the new car. (NARA.)

Here are other innovations made at the Camp Edwards convalescent hospital. They are escape chutes for patients who occupied the second floors. (NARA.)

The hospitals did not only serve
GIs from the Second World War,
it was reactivated to service those
from the Korean Conflict. Talking
with 2nd Lt. Leo B. Elderidge of
North Larrence, New York, a double
amputee, is secretary of the army
Frank Pace Jr. The nurse is Capt.
Sue G. Carey. This photograph was
taken August 13, 1951. (NARA.)

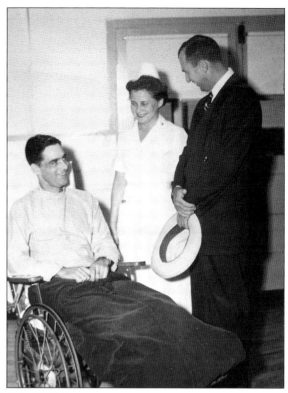

Cpl. Joseph Leblanc of Lynn is
receiving cigarettes and other gifts
from Mrs. Roy A. Berg of Falmouth,
Massachusetts, a member of the
Grey Lady volunteer organization.
Corporal Leblanc was a member
of the 1st Cavalry when he was
wounded at Inchon, Korea.
The date of this photograph is
December 4, 1950. (NARA.)

Hundreds of wood-frame buildings, thousands of men, as well as the ranges where live fire took place near wooded areas required that a well-trained and equipped fire department be established on the post. Here one can see trucks with ladders for the buildings. There is also a truck with a frame built to protect it in the woods. (MNG.)

This guesthouse was used for family and friends when they came for a visit. Normally a visit was for three days, but if a person was in the hospital, the stay was extended until any danger was passed. The cost of a night started at 75¢, but rose to $1 before war's end. Only 50 guests could be accommodated, so advance reservations were required. A dayroom was provided for guests. (MNG.)

There were many shops and storerooms built in the troop area of the camp to repair and modify equipment. This is one of them as it looked on August 13, 1942. (NARA.)

Soldiers from Camp Edwards were a large presence on the Upper Cape. In this photograph, taken in the 1940s at the Woods Hole railroad station, the soldiers and their jeeps and trucks do not seem to be noticed by passengers who just got off an afternoon train. (NARA.)

Trains brought nearly everything to Camp Edwards, including the boats for the amphibian engineers. (NARA.)

The tents on Washburn Island were for the infantry divisions, and amphibious engineers camped and trained in order to learn to make the successful landings on the enemy beaches. (NARA.)

This is the PX on Washburn Island, just about 5 miles from the main camp located on Nantucket Sound by Waquoit Bay. (NARA.)

Photographs were taken from the water tower on October 10, 1944. This shows the company areas that make up the battalions and the regiments. (NARA.)

This view shows post office No. 2 and the bank in the foreground. (NARA.)

This view shows the Central Fire Station in the foreground. (NARA.)

The embarkation area was where soldiers arrived or departed Camp Edwards. They came and went by either units or small groups. The beginning and the end of their memories of army life on Cape Cod were here. Whole divisions, such as the 26th Infantry, departed for the war on trains. The 36th Division arrived from Texas August 14–21, 1942. It took 40 trains to get the division to Cape Cod from April 1 to 21, 1943. They boarded trains to New York to board ships that took them to North Africa. The 82nd Airborne Division came here on their way to Anzio, Italy. The Women's Auxiliary Corps came in 1943. Casualties from Europe were shipped here for convalescence. Trains to other hospitals for specialized treatment sent some away. German prisoners arrived after the North African Campaign. The 45th Division from Oklahoma/Texas was here in 1943 for amphibious training. Author and cartoonist Bill Mauldin came to Camp Edwards with the 45th Division. He went on to create the most famous two cartoon soldiers of the war, Willie and Joe. (MNG.)

Three

TRAINING

Camp Falmouth – 1938

To say that the U.S. Army was not in fighting trim in the years leading up to World War II is not quite a stretch. The Great Depression had both bolstered the number of Americans in the military and raised retention rates, since leaving the military meant looking for a job elsewhere, and created armament shortages that hindered training. There were plenty of troops, but pretending to fire wooden replicas of machine guns hardly equaled the experience of true firing that would prepare a soldier for war. The coming of World War II further expanded the troop base, but also led to an unprecedented industrial growth in armaments production. With real guns and a real cause for which to fight, America's fighting men would soon be whipped into shape. (MANGHA.)

The obstacles that the average GI would face would be various in both severity and dangerousness. In this image, troops train from an antiaircraft unit run and leap to clear a wall. Ropes hang from the top for those soldiers not tall enough to reach it under their own strength and speed. Full packs and shoulder-slung rifles added to the burden. (FSA.)

Belly crawling through an "asparagus patch" might look like an easy task, but the goal was to contort one's body between posts laid out in a straight line. If two millennia of warfare in the Western world have proven anything, it is that soldiers can expect to become well acquainted with mud at some time in their military careers. (FSA.)

Almost as if taken purposely in slow-motion capture, the antiaircraft troops demonstrate the proper leaping and landing techniques for jumping a chasm. In this case, sandbags cushion the blow. In combat, such niceties were a pipe dream. (FSA.)

One might ask, "What benefit would an antiaircraft soldier gain from such training?" While the obstacle course at the Camp Edwards antiaircraft training center was not job-specific, it was designed to strengthen the muscles and mental acuity of any soldier. Whether advancing or retreating across a battle-scarred landscape, soldiers would face obstacles of untold varieties. (FSA.)

Leading by example has been a standard strategy for military officers through the ages. Soldiers uninspired by their leadership cannot be effective compared to those men and women who subscribe strongly to the exhortations of their leader. Quotes from great leaders ring through the ages, but perhaps nothing fit the World War II American serviceman better than the words of Capt. Henry P. Crowe. On January 13, 1943, while leading a charge against entrenched Japanese troops on Guadalcanal, he yelled to his men, "You'll never get a Purple Heart hiding in a foxhole! Follow me!" Here three officers training with the antiaircraft troops "show 'em how it's done." At the conclusion of the training center's grueling obstacle course, they scramble up the face of a 6-foot wall and, releasing a primal battlefield scream, cross to the other side. (FSA.)

Through all of the obstacles shown in these images, including this steeplechase vault over a 5-foot fence, troops were expected to maintain balance, keep their equipment, and be ready to stand and fight once it was completed. The target time was three and a half minutes. (FSA.)

In times of war as well as peace, allies share resources. At right, three members of the Greek Army offer a salute. From left to right are Pvt. James Bezirgianidis, Thomas Harris (née Hanozoes), and Damainos Daykos. (FSA.)

Of course not everything that had to be taught and learned in relation to war could be done through physical exercise. Numerous knowledge standards had to be met, some services-wide, and some job, rank, or rate specific. Classroom time was as important as a charge through an obstacle course or an hour on a firing range. Considering the multiple theaters of the current war and the copious styles of landscapes and terrains into which troops would be inserted—usually to fight an entrenched enemy well familiar with the land—map reading was a basic requisite skill. Here 1st Lt. Nathaniel J. Young Jr. offers a course. Young graduated from Boston Latin Academy in 1938 and Harvard in 1942, served in intelligence during the war, graduated from Harvard Law in 1948, and became a leading lawyer in Massachusetts. (FDM.)

As noted earlier in the book, marching was a standard facet of military life. Here the 137th Antiaircraft Artillery (AAA) marches to class across snowy terrain. (FDM.)

The 137th AAA had an ignominious start to life, partially forming at other bases, believing it would be the 133rd, transferring to Camp Edwards, and finally being assigned a number on June 10, 1943. Once the unit had enough men—which took much longer than expected—it began a 21-week mobilization training program, or MTP. (FDM.)

The 137th AAA was one of those units that was either lucky or unlucky, depending on how one looked at it. In a time when every military man knew it was a badge of honor to state he had been in combat, despite the long-term ramifications that could result from the action, the 137th trained and trained but never traveled overseas. (FDM.)

Instead, theirs was a life of marches and study, of inspections, and eventually live firing exercises. One man, Charles Stern, kept his memoirs and said that the only thing that made getting through the days easy was the fact that night was coming, until the command began the practice of night firing at Wellfleet. (FDM.)

"Some of the hikes were pretty grueling," said Charles Stern in his book *The History of Battery "A," 137 Anti-Aircraft Artillery Gun Bn.*, "and the old feet and legs got stiff; some men even rode home in the dog wagon in shame. All in all we did get in shape, and the hikes and exercises grew easier. When the physical proficiency of 'A' Battery was checked at the end of MTP, we were 97% Charles Atlas." Civilian life had been left behind at the end of the 21-week preparation. "MTP was a confusing period, full of backaches and headaches, but it did change us into soldiers. When we had finished . . . we were ready for almost anything. Instinctively we walked with a thirty-inch step and were nauseated by the sight of a necktie not tucked in between the second and third shirt buttons." (FDM.)

Machine gunners, expected to be among the shortest-lived combatants on any battlefield, had grounds of their own as well. Here Pvt. Armand R. Valcourt (left) is being coached by Sgt. Paul Levasseur on firing the .50-caliber machine gun as Lt. Col. John J. Mullin looks on, on August 17, 1950. (NARA.)

Even tank crews found room to maneuver at Camp Edwards. Here members of the 321st Cavalry Squadron serve as the crew of a M-24 light tank during an August 1948 encampment. From left to right, Lt. Andrew M. Moodie is the assistant driver, Lt. James Chekos is the instructor, Lt. Rollin C. Wilcox of Medfield is tank commander, and Capt. Leonard H. Kieley of Bedford is the driver. (NARA.)

Whether coming from the muzzle of a cannon, the boom of a hand-tossed grenade, or the upright rifle of an antiaircraft gun, as seen in this 1951 image, the sounds of war rang out across the Upper Cape regularly during wartime. (MNG.)

A major component of artillery training is learning to train sights on distant targets for maximum effect. Here Lt. Robert Allman of Wakefield, M.Sgt. Santo J. Cardello (with walkie-talkie), and M.Sgt. E. Cirigliano of Medford, all with the 421st Field Artillery Group of the Massachusetts Officer Reserve Corps, take a reading on July 14, 1950. (NARA.)

These artillerymen knew that should all else fail, they would revert to foot soldiers on the field of battle. Here members of the 421st Field Artillery group practice firing their M-1 rifles during an August 1948 encampment. From left to right are Sgt. Parker G. McCartney of Wellesley; Sgt. John J. Gallivan of Jamaica Plain; Cpl. John Cronin of Milton, firing; and Sgt. Alfred A. Alvarez of Chelsea, coaching. (NARA.)

Warring armies take advantage of every natural advantage they can, from hilltops for commanding views of terrain, to dense jungles for camouflage, to the darkness of night. During their preparation for war, the men of the 137th AAA learned to fire their guns at night at an off base extension of Camp Edwards, Camp Wellfleet. (MNG.)

World War II became a showcase for jeeps, especially after the Germans made their way across Europe, blitzkrieg-like, in small, fast vehicles. The military chose three designs for what would become known as jeeps, ultimately awarding Ford a contract in November 1941 to produce 15,000 Willys Overland jeeps for the war. Here a Bantam GPV proves its worth off the main roads at Camp Edwards. (MANGHA.)

Despite the massive amount of land taken for the creation of the Massachusetts Military Reservation, certain trainings required varied grounds. In this image, vehicles head across a pontoon bridge towards Camp Washburn on Washburn Island in East Falmouth in 1942. The 594th Engineer Boat and Shore Regiment trained here for less than a year. (NARA.)

North, at the extreme western end of Sandy Neck Beach, Scorton Neck in Sandwich was used as an antiaircraft artillery training area. (MNG.)

BIVOUAC AREA
1P WELLFLEET - MASS.

The 137th AAA also used Camp Wellfleet. The unit bivouacked on the beach for the first time between October 18 and November 2, 1943, and conducted three more firings between then and April 1, 1944. Charles Stern remembered those first days as being less than invigorating: "When the guns finally arrived at the firing point, we found that only the M4 tractors could pull them into position in the sand. Consequently our first day—and it was our last good firing day for some time—was spent in setting down the battery . . . At night we pitched pup tents in the sand and soon learned that in Cape Cod weather double shelter tents have many advantages over the conventional model. During the next few days we waited for a break in the sky. Sometimes it rained, and sometimes the low ceiling precluded firing, but there was no break. We tried training, but there was little we could do on Wellfleet's wind-swept bluffs." (MANGHA.)

Camp Edwards
Well Fleet

One wonders, with the cacophony of an artillery firing range, whether or not this soldier would have awoken to the sound of the hammer striking his helmet. Practical jokes in the military were a fantastic way to ease the tension, boredom, and frustration of training. (MNG.)

Hand-to-hand combat is always a possibility in wartime, especially when it comes to subduing your own men. At left, on July 10, 1950, Lt. Carl Catalano demonstrates the use of a nightstick on Sgt. Samuel Saracen for the members of the 307th Military Police Battalion. Should an American soldier become rowdy during leave time, these men needed to be able to control any situation. (NARA.)

Two unnamed soldiers practice a knee and chin jab on August 28, 1942. (NARA.)

During this scene in 1942, Pvt. James N. Kelley and Sgt. Tom S. Whitney, both U.S. Army Rangers, demonstrate how to silence a Nazi sentry. Kelley grabs the rifle of the sentry, played by Cpl. Lloyd D. Lamascus, while Whitney clamps his gloved hand over his mouth. (NARA.)

Of course, American soldiers might be on the receiving end of the same treatment. Here on July 22, 1950, Capt. Roger Brady describes to members of the 366th Criminal Investigation Division the possible foul play evidence to be found around the body of a mock murder victim. (NARA.)

The American military saved many lives during the Great Depression, offering men of fighting age willing to enlist a safe place to sleep and three square meals a day. While volunteerism lasted into the World War II years, spiking on December 8, 1941, involuntary service soon followed. Military service for a generation of American men became a rite of passage. Here members of the 307th Military Police Battalion, Lt. Dennis Dempsey, Maj. J. B. Bennett, Maj. Samuel A. Abrahams, Capt. G. E. Levesque, Lt. M. F. Sheehan, Maj. L. C. McNeil, Maj. Walter J. Fowler, and Capt. N. J. Vickers, raise pistols on July 15, 1950, as part of their training. They stood as part of a long line of men willing to lay down their lives for their country should the call sound. (NARA.)

Four

THE MOCK
GERMAN VILLAGE

In 1943, it was evident that sooner or later American troops would be fighting in Germany. Therefore a mock German village was built in the range area of Camp Edwards in order to train solders in urban warfare. The 150th Combat Engineer Battalion, made up of all New England personnel who were training at Fort Devens, were selected to build it. Working in two shifts, they accomplished the task in three days. (MNG.)

Deutschedorf had three streets: Rommel Strasse, Freidrich Strasse, and Wilhelm Strasse. The three soldiers in the left foreground are standing in the main intersection of the three streets. The street leading to the small building in the background is Rommel Strasse, and the small building's sign says it is the "birthplace" of the fuhrer. The building is clearly a latrine. Directly behind the "birthplace" is the Gestapo headquarters. Other buildings included a beer garden, a restaurant, a school, a bank, the mayor's house, a baker, butcher shop, barbershop, a theater, and dwellings. Most of the buildings did not have a rear wall, making it much like a Hollywood set. (FDM.)

The engineers are still putting finishing touches on the village. The barbershop has a pole and its sign. More than just German signs, details such as flower boxes, fences, and birdhouses were all added to give the appearance of a real village. (FDM.)

The *Boston Post* on July 19, 1943, published an article describing the village and the training procedure. Soldiers would approach the village along Wilhelm Strasse alert for snipers. An observer would let a hidden operator know where a soldier was, and he would pull targets. The targets would be silhouettes often of German chancellor Adolf Hitler, which would show up at a window, behind a door or a fence, or even on a roof. (FDM.)

The village name was posted as the soldiers came in to the village. The schoolhouse is across the street. (FDM.)

Every village had a barbershop, and every GI needed to get a haircut, and often. In this photograph, it looks like members of the 150th Engineer Combat Battalion are lined up waiting for their turn with the barber. (FDM.)

A favorite place with soldiers of all nations and all times is the beer hall. This is Deutschedorf's own beer hall and beer garden. Note the sign over the front door of the foamy beverage and the proud constructors of this local bar. After building this village in only three days, these soldiers are properly ready for a beer break. (FDM.)

Gestapo headquarters was located just behind the birthplace of the fuhrer. The GIs are having a little fun with their mock Fascist salute. The word *Gestapo* is a contraction of "Geheim Staatspolizert," which translates to "secret state police." It is unlikely that a small village would have had a Gestapo station, but it would have had a local police station. (FDM.)

The fuhrer has finished his business inside his "birthplace" and makes a Fascist salute to his followers as he stands by the front door. (FDM.)

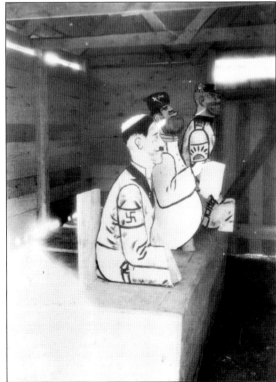

Inside the "birthplace" (the latrine) of the fuhrer are Fascist leaders. Adolph Hitler is in the first hole and Tojo, the Japanese prime minister, is in the last hole. The person in the middle is harder to identify. He could be Draza Mlhallovic, the Chetnik leader in the Serbian section of Yugoslavia. The Chetniks were considered pro-Axis. (FDM.)

At the south end of the runway a German POW camp was built. This camp housed as many as 2,000 men. The prisoners were captured in the North African Campaign that ended in May 1943. They worked on and off the base. Building projects and farmwork took up much of their time. The harvesting of lumber from the trees blown down by the hurricane of September 1944 was assigned to the POWs. Over 8 million feet of lumber was salvaged by the prisoners under the supervision of U.S. Army personnel knowledgeable of the industry. (NARA.)

The pictures in this series are of POWs harvesting the trees following the hurricane of September 1944 and were taken September 12, 1945, by the Army Signal Corps. A production line has been set up to take whole cut logs to a sawmill to be cut into proper lengths. (NARA.)

Logs of various sizes are loaded onto a truck to be carried to the various sawmills to be cut into boards. (NARA.)

In the center of this photograph is 1st Lt. Harold Snyder of McMillan, Michigan. He was the assistant officer in charge of the hurricane lumber project. On the left is a German POW, no doubt English-speaking and acting as a foreman. On the right is a military police guard. Maj. E. G. Hamlin, who had 30 years of experience in the lumber business, was put in charge of the overall operation. (NARA.)

This crew of prisoners is collecting scrap ends of lumber and taking them out of the yard where they stored the boards that have been cut. (NARA.)

This is one of the four sawmills that was set up at Camp Edwards. The sawmills were sent from the state of Washington. The prisoners worked eight hours a day. By the time of this photograph, 20,000 feet of lumber had been cut, well on their way to the 8 million feet cut on Cape Cod in 1944–1945. All the lumber on Camp Edwards was cut by the POWs. It would be interesting to know if any structures still survive with POW boards. (NARA.)

WESTERN UNION

A. N. WILLIAMS
PRESIDENT

The .... STANDARD TIME .... of origin. Time of receipt is STANDARD TIME at point of destination

WA23 DL=CENTERVILLE MASS 5 956A

CONGRESSMAN CHARLES L GIFFORD=

US CONGRESS WASHDC=

WOULD LIKE TO ENTER STRONG PROTEST WITH YOU IN BEHALF OF
SMALL BUSINESS FOLKS WHO HAVE MILLIONS OF DOLLARS INVESTE
ON CAPE COD AGAINST THE ARMIES HAVING A STOCKADE PRISON C
AT CAMP EDWARDS FOR PRISONERS OF WAR IN THE HEART OF NEW
ENGLANDS FINEST SUMMER RESORT WHY DOESNT THE ARMY INSTEAD
MAKE IT A HOSPITAL CAMP AND LET OUR HOMECOMING BOYS ENJOY
AND BE COMFORTED BY CAPE COD SEASHORE AND SEA BREEZES=
    JOHN J PENDERGAST.

THE COMPANY WILL APPRECIATE SUGGESTIONS FROM ITS PATRONS CONCERNING ITS SERVICE

Cranberry growers and other farmers who had shortage of labor may have been happy to have POWs to help with their crops. However, not everyone, as can be seen by this telegram, was happy to have the German prisoners on the Cape. There were more than 200 prisoners engaged in the tree-salvaging operation. (NARA.)

Five

AN AVENUE AND
NOT A ROADBLOCK

The Amphibious Training Command was established May 20, 1942, at Camp Edwards. Its mission was to develop procedures for large and small amphibious operations. It also was responsible for recruiting and training personnel for the command and to develop equipment for amphibious operations. (NARA.)

Col. Daniel Noce (promoted to brigadier general on July 27, 1942) was appointed as the first commander of the Amphibious Training Command. Within 15 days, then general Noce had established and activated the 1st and 2nd Engineer Amphibian Brigades (later known as Engineer Special Brigades). Personnel were recruited as well as boats acquired. The command soon changed its name to the Amphibious Training Center. (NARA.)

The grand question to be answered was how to get men and supplies ashore safely during battle. The men trained at several camps, including Camp Washburn on Washburn Island in Waquoit Bay, Falmouth; Camp Canduit in Cotuit; and Camp Havedoneit in Osterville. This camp was located on the property of the Crosby Yacht Yard. Beach training and equipment testing was done on Sandy Neck, Barnstable, off Provincetown, and other locations on the Cape. In order for the Amphibious Training Command to reach its goal of recruiting and training a large number of personnel to operate, repair, and be able to land forces on enemy beaches, they recruited experienced personnel from the Coast Guard, navy, and marines, as well as British commandos. An advertisement campaign to enlist knowledgeable personnel from civilian life was launched in boating magazines, as well as notices to the working water trades. Yachtsmen with college backgrounds were considered for officers, and lobstermen, boat pilots, and the like were considered for noncommissioned officers. The campaign was so successful that many skilled people enlisted directly into the command. However, they lacked military training and had to take this training before they could function in the command. (NARA.)

This DUKW, or "Duck," is driving over pierced steel planking (PSP), also known as a Somerfield Net. This was used to strengthen the ground to support heavy equipment passing over it. It was used in hastily built airfields during World War II. Both the DUKW and the planking were tested in the waters and beaches of Cape Cod. (NARA.)

The World War II DUKW ("D" for the year 1942, "U" for utility-amphibious, "K" means all-wheel drive, and "W" for two powered rear axles) was designed around this General Motors truck from its Yellow Truck and Coach division. This was the 2.5-ton standard military truck. (NARA.)

This is a photograph of General Motors representatives testing the DUKW in a lake in the Midwest. This image was included in the proposal that was sent to the Amphibious Training Center for their tests and consideration of the vehicle. The chief designer was Rod Stephens Jr., a yacht designer for Sparkman, Stephens, Inc. His staff may be onboard for this demonstration. (NARA.)

Here is more of the design team of the DUKW. There is a story that the DUKW was rejected for the military until one rescued a Coast Guard Auxiliary boat *Yaw Rose* after it was stuck on a sandbar off Provincetown during a storm. However, it is more likely it was approved after rigorous sea trials in Chesapeake Bay and the open sea, as well as off-road tests at Fort Belvoir and loading tests at Forts Eustis and Story, all in Virginia. They were used and tested on Cape Cod for the Amphibious Training Center. (NARA.)

Chris-Craft Boats, the pleasure boatbuilder, provided more than 10,000 landing craft to the government in World War II. LCPLs (Landing Craft Personnel, Large)—there is one 36-foot-long landing craft in this photograph—were made by Chris-Craft based on the Higgins boat design. They are shallow drafted, built of steel and wood, and were the main way of transporting troops to the enemy beaches of World War II. (NARA.)

After the North African invasion (November 8, 1942), in which the Engineer Amphibian Troops took part, the mission of the Engineer Special Brigades was explained to the public. First they were to take combat troops over the water to the enemy-held shore. Second, they were to capture the enemy beach and to organize it to facilitate combat troops moving inland. Third was to evacuate the wounded, salvage equipment, and transport prisoners to the ships offshore. Fourth was to resupply the combat units on the beach by water. (NARA.)

The amphibian troops tested and experimented with many types of ground-strengthening devices to enable combat vehicles and equipment to move over sandy beaches to the inland. They tried products from simple fencing to heavy airfield gridding. This view shows an Irving Grid, a material used in constructing semipermanent airfields. (NARA.)

The troops are testing and practicing the moving of a semitrailer with a crane onto a Cape Cod beach. The different conditions of beaches and the sand of the beach, coupled with the need to act carefully and with skill under enemy fire, predicated the need to get the action right the first time in combat. (NARA.)

Supplies and equipment arriving on the beach called for an easy and fast means of accomplishment. The need to salvage equipment from the beach could be achieved by such things as a marine railway, as seen in this photograph. (NARA.)

This 4-ton truck is stuck in a swamp on Sandy Neck. There was much at stake for the amphibious engineers. If the first truck off a landing craft became stuck, the mission could end in disaster. (NARA.)

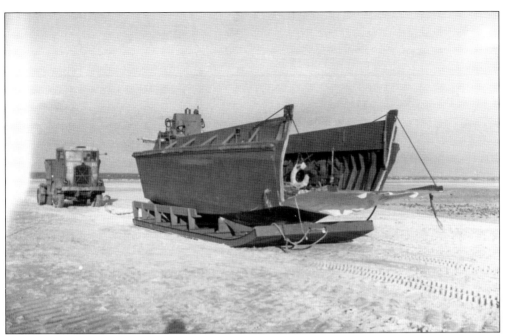

Skid trailers were another way to get equipment up and down the beach. (NARA.)

The men in this picture are attempting to pull this landing craft onto the beach by means of a marine rollerway. This is a device that has two rails, and on the rails are wheels. The boat will move while resting on the wheels onto the beach. (NARA.)

A truck is in place to pull the boat up the rollerway. The men are on either side to guide. The man with his hands out will signal if the boat is precariously leaning to one side or the other. The marine rollerway was one of the ways to move things onto the beach until a port and docking facility was available. (NARA.)

This image gives a view of the rollers of the marine rollerway. Amphibious engineers had many options to get equipment on and off the beach. Which one was to be used depended on the conditions when invasions took place. (NARA.)

In this case, wheels have been added to the landing craft. The wheels are detachable in this operation. (NARA.)

The wheels on this landing are retractable, yet not detachable. It is possible that all the tactics that were developed and taught were never used. Yet it is better to have the experience and the options, considering the importance amphibian operations held in the Second World War. (NARA.)

Not all the equipment that had to be brought on and off the beach was large and heavy. These torpedoes are in towing position, ready to be pulled out to a ship or boat. The people who had cottages on Sandy Neck or other nearby beaches were certainly entertained during the war years with all the activity of the amphibious engineers. (NARA.)

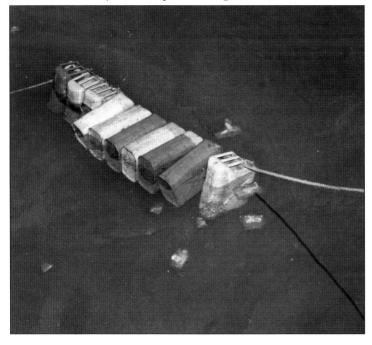

The simplest way to move things in water was to tie them together and pull them with a line, as these jerry cans demonstrate. (NARA.)

The Engineer Amphibian Brigades were designed to support the landing of an infantry division. To this end, a brigade consisted of a headquarters company and three boat and shore regiments, a boat repair battalion, a medical battalion, a signal company, and an ordnance company, as well as a quartermaster company. This is the quartermaster at work, unloading supplies to be taken on to the beach. Longshoremen and stevedores were recruited into the amphibious engineers for their expertise and knowledge in this type of work. The training in this photograph is the unloading of supplies on pallets. An infantry division needed from 500 to 700 tons of supplies a day. This ranged from ammunition, food, and medical supplies, to all those things that an army in the field needed. The LST (Landing Ship, Tank) was developed at the same time to deliver tanks and trucks to the beach as well as DUKWs, which were put into service unloading materials from supply ships. (NARA.)

Unloading small pallets from a ship in various sea conditions required training and skill. Adding to the ordeal, the enemy was expected to be firing on the beachhead and invasion fleet. (NARA.)

In this case, the cargo net is putting the supplies on a float. From the float, the supplies will be loaded into a landing craft. (NARA.)

The landing craft is in position to have the material from the net packed in it. Note the beach cottages. This is Sandy Neck, Cape Cod. (NARA.)

Another cargo net load is being lowered onto a float to be packed into a landing craft and taken to the beach. Sandy Neck Beach was used often for the training of the amphibious engineers. In this photograph, more cottages are seen. (NARA.)

As the supplies landed on the beach they had to be organized for the distribution to the troops. This appears to be early in the beach organization and distribution process. Note the tables where the organization could be centered and controlled. (NARA.)

Sometimes heavy equipment was called for to flatten out supply dumps, in order to efficiently store and distribute supplies to the combat units engaging the enemy. (NARA.)

This aerial photograph shows the beach covered with the supplies that the amphibious engineers brought and organized there. This operation alone is a major undertaking but is only one of the missions of these seaborne engineers. (NARA.)

Once the supplies were landed on the beach and organized, the next mission was to move them out and get them to the troops. (NARA.)

4. 1319-5 Experimental - 1st Boat - "Handy Willie". General view, port quarter aft.

Part of the mission for the amphibious engineers was to retrieve equipment from the beach, and this called for some innovation. A landing craft was turned into a boat that became very useful. Designated experimental and named *Handy Willie*, this boat evolved as it was used to complete many salvage tasks. (NARA.)

16. R-1352-4 Experimental - 1st Boat - "Handy Willie". Method used in the surf. Salvage Boat held securely in relation to the beached boat by means of the anchor aft and lines forward through the ramp fairleads, back to the niggerheads on the hoist through the bollard and snatch block system. If the beached boat were imbedded in the sand a lift with the boom could be taken to break the suction. The equipment and the operation is the same for the Final Design - 2nd Boat - "Handy Jimmie".

Here one can read the original caption of a photograph of *Handy Willie*, taken at the time of the development of this craft into a suitable salvage boat. (NARA.)

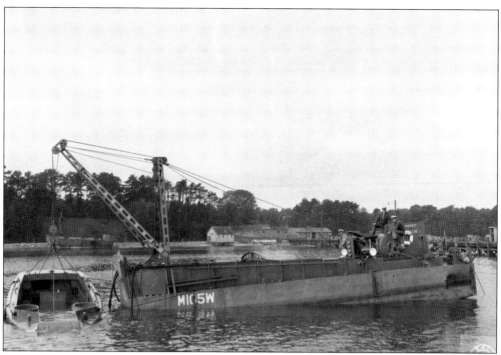

In this photograph, *Handy Willie* is retrieving a sunken boat. All of the tests and trials of *Handy Willie* added to the knowledge that was responsible for producing a final salvage boat design. (NARA.)

27. 1352-15 Experimental - 1st Boat - "Handy Willie". Salvage Boat performing a towing operation. The Final Design - 2nd Boat - "Handy Jimmie" is appreciably superior for this operation due to the increased power and maneuverability - 2 Gray - 225 H.P. Engines of opposite rotation as against 2 Buda 105 H.P. engines of the same rotation.

In this photograph, *Handy Jimmie* is standing by as good old *Handy Willie* performs a towing task. *Jimmie* replaced *Willie*. The development of the salvage boat was a sample of the type of experimental work the amphibious engineers achieved while training at Camp Edwards and nearby beaches. (NARA.)

The army liked the idea of having an amphibious jeep. Marmon-Herrington built one on the standard jeep models by Ford, known as a SEEP (Sea Jeep). The vehicle pictured here was the *Aqua Cheetah*. Roger W. Hofheins designed it, and it was built by the Amphibian Car Corporation, Buffalo, New York. Its military supply catalog number was G552, half-ton truck. (NARA.)

The amphibious engineers tested the *Aqua Cheetah*. It does not show up other than in prototypes, of which there were three variants. The SEEP, built on the Ford jeep model, did not have high production numbers due to performance faults. It took on water in choppy seas and was heavier than the standard jeep on land. (NARA.)

The photograph shows the *Aqua Cheetah* doing well in the water. The waves in this photograph are not high. (NARA.)

This is a photograph of the *Aqua Cheetah* returning to the beach after her sea trials, and the event is being recorded. Like the SEEP, this vehicle had issues with its performance on land. After these trials, the *Aqua Cheetah* slipped into the backwaters of obscurity. (NARA.)

Working in wet and cold conditions under fire was a motivation to seek as much protection as was practical for the soldiers of the amphibious engineers. This is the model S1 Sea Suit, which was tested for use in wet conditions. (NARA.)

Another suit that was tested was the Liberty Sea Suit. (NARA.)

Crosby's Yacht Yard is the subject of this photograph. A landing craft in the background is pulled up on the slipway. In the foreground is one of the cabin cruisers used by the amphibious engineers. This boat strongly resembles the one being pulled out of the water by *Handy Willie* in a previous photograph. (NARA.)

"D-Days" and "H-Hours" would be future watchwords for America's fighting men, but training for those moments was already taking place in 1942. While landing on a beachhead and delivering troops and supplies ashore was one aspect of the amphibious assault process, surviving the assault and driving the enemy back would take more than good seamanship and well-tested landing equipment. Here in a dramatic moment in July 1942, which previewed innumerable landings on European and Pacific shores, one soldier lays across barbed wire while another uses that man's back as a springboard to bypass the impediment. (NARA.)

The men of the Amphibious Training Command also exercised what would one day be called "brown water ops (operations)," river-based assaults in small boats. This crew is in rowing position on dry land in a 10-man rubber boat, mounted with a .30-caliber machine gun on August 28, 1942. (NARA.)

In order to replicate closely grown European forests, the Amphibious Training Command took felled trees and stood them upright. Soldiers practiced moving amongst them in this 1942 image. (NARA.)

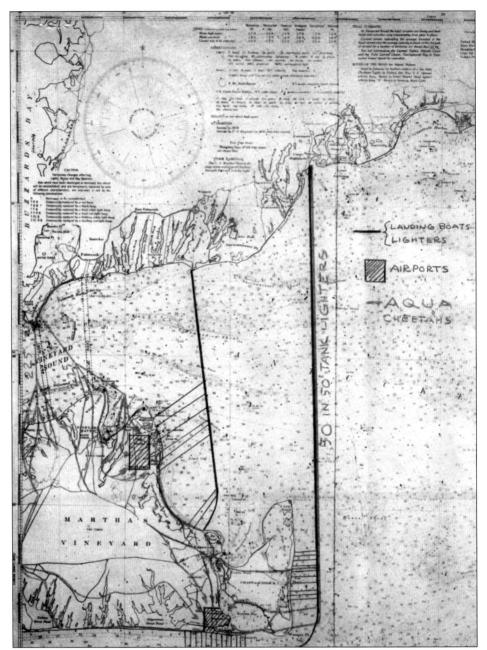

October 2–3, 1942, the 1st and 2nd Engineer Amphibian Brigades prepared for a classified training exercise, the invasion of Martha's Vineyard. The 36th Infantry Division was the force that was to liberate the Vineyard from the "enemy." Above is the chart for this invasion. The troops got in their boats with their equipment the night before the training. They hit the beach at first light. As they approached the shore, they came out of the night in silence, right on time. Lt. Gen. Lesley J. McNair, who was in charge of all U.S. Army training, was an observer. He was later killed in France. Even though the exercise was classified, many people from the Vineyard were out to see it. Paratroops were landed and air units were preparing the way. The "enemy" was defending the airport as well as the rest of the island. (NARA.)

The Martha's Vineyard "invasion" was considered a success. Even so, not everything went as planned. A landing craft carrying 25 men caught fire. The men jumped overboard. The landing craft continued speeding along and became a potential menace. A boat crew commanded by 1st Lt. Ernest B. Heuter was able to rescue all the men from the burning craft. Then, as Heuter's boat caught up to the burning runaway boat, he leapt into the latter craft, put out the fire, and stopped its forward progress. First Lt. Ernest B. Heuter, mission leader of Red 2 on October 2, 1942, received the Soldier's Medal for rescuing the 25 men from the burning landing craft. The landing craft was retrieved and repaired and put back into service. (NARA.)

The uniqueness of the training of the Amphibious Training Command and the other units passing through Camp Edwards brought Secretary of War Henry L. Stimson to witness it firsthand. In this picture, Stimson stands second from left, sharing a word with a British artillery officer. To his right stand Lt. Gen. Leslie McNair, Maj. Gen. Douglas T. Greene, and Brig. Gen. Morris C. Handwerk. (NARA.)

The global scope of World War II meant that American soldiers would have to be prepared to fight in every climate and every habitat, from the desert to the tundra. These men modeled various looks of the American fighting man in the 1940s. (NARA.)

The fact that half of the war would be fought in the Pacific theater prompted the military to experiment with different types of jungle camouflage, as modeled here by the camp's camouflage school in 1942. (NARA.)

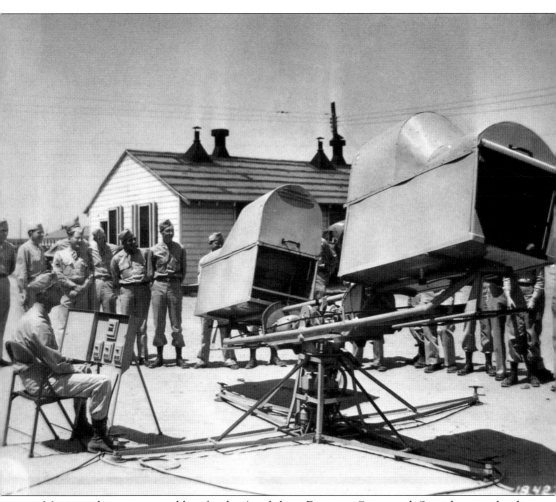

Motion sickness was a problem for the Amphibian Engineer Command. Seasickness in landing crafts was high, and this caused a loss of efficiency. General Noce asked command surgeon Col. L. L. Barrow and his staff to study the causes of seasickness and seek a remedy that would not lower a person's awareness or reduce his abilities. Rides in boats under various conditions and durations were employed to study seasickness but were ineffective due to the fact it was impossible to reproduce similar conditions. A machine that could simulate waterborne motion under laboratory conditions was designed, pictured above. A model of its design was produced, and the 411th Engineers Base Shop Battalion built it. It was installed at Camp Edwards Williams Hospital. (NARA.)

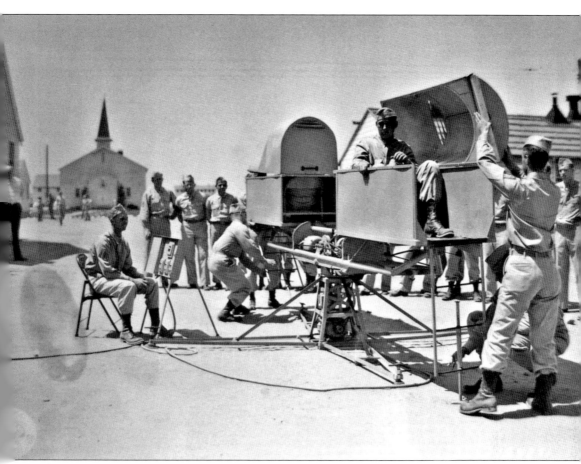

The machine could accommodate two men, one on each end of the apparatus. All the basic movements of a boat on water could be reproduced by this machine: pitch, the seesaw motion from stem to stern, roll or partial rotation of the boat on its bow and stern axis, and yaw, a sidewise motion. The Motion-Sickness Machine was put into action on February 1, 1943. The results of the study were a pharmaceutical remedy for motion sickness. The remedy, according to the study report, was 100 percent effective in preventing severe and moderate motion sickness and 90 percent effective in preventing mild motion sickness. The report prescribed the method of taking the "pill," one a half hour before embarkation, one at the moment of embarkation, and one every four hours from then on. The development of a preventative medicine for motion was considered a great achievement of the Amphibian Engineer Command. The official report cautions "no publicity on this subject will be released for the present, since it is feared that knowledge of the drug might be of value to the enemy." (ACE.)

General Noce had high expectations of his boatmen and all other men in the amphibious engineers. He addressed his troops, saying that they should consider the water they had to cross, in order to land on enemy shore, an "avenue and not an obstacle." He went on to say that a disciplined amphibious force that is well trained and equipped could change an enemy flank protected by water from the strongest flank to the weakest flank. The 1st Engineer Special Brigade formed at Camp Edwards on June 15, 1942, and left for England, ready for combat, just a month and a half later. General Noce's men and command theories were tested in both theaters. (NARA.)

Six

OTIS FIELD

Following Charles Lindbergh's transatlantic journey in 1927, aviation caught on as a pastime for many Americans in the 1930s, leading to the construction of many small regional airports. When the Massachusetts Military Reservation was laid out between 1935 and 1940, plans included two 500-foot grass runways to be known as Otis Field. Lt. Frank Otis—a pilot and renowned Boston City Hospital surgeon, shown here with an Curtiss XO-12—died on a cross-country training mission in his Douglas O-46A on January 11, 1937, while serving with the 101st Observation Squadron. (MANGHA.)

In 1940, the Massachusetts National Guard's 101st Observation Squadron, then serving at Jeffries Field in East Boston on the site of today's Logan International Airport, was inducted into federal service and transferred to Otis Field. After 1943, the base fell under the umbrella of Naval Air Station Quonset Point, Rhode Island, being named Naval Auxiliary Air Facility Otis. Under the guise of the navy, the base took a lead role in antisubmarine patrols of nearby waters. Photographer Walter Fleming, who shot aerials from a North American O-47, said of this photograph, "Stare at this a couple of minutes and grab a parachute. You'll probably feel as though you were falling. I did." (MANGHA.)

The construction of large wooden hangars for use by military aviation units was not, at first, necessary in a world already accustomed to the use of metals in construction. But as the war advanced and the United States began rationing many items for the war effort, scrap metals were at the top of that list. Construction of military buildings with wood, like the original Otis Field hangar, served the country in two ways. (MANGHA.)

Within a few years of the opening of Otis Field, scenes like this flight line of P-47 Thunderbolts in 1948 would become a normal sight. The Thunderbolt, or "Thud," was the heaviest and largest single-engine fighter plane in World War II; however, it was beloved by those men who flew it for its rugged durability and ability to take a pounding during a dogfight. (MANGHA.)

The 26th Aviation Division's photography section certainly knew how to pose for a picture. This one was taken on July 22, 1938. (MANGHA.)

The officers of the 26th Aviation Division also knew how to strike a pose. In classic military fashion, this image came only with last names. From left to right are (first row) M. Hollidge, Sprague, Richardson, Stinson, Hodge, Edson, Cruff, Baker, and Griffin; (second row) Ashworth, McNeill, Shaw, Flinn, Keith, Thompson, Roullard, C. Hollidge, Jakeway, and Beck. (MANGHA.)

As needs changed, so, too, did Otis Field. The old turf runways were replaced by concrete in 1942, and the following year, those new runways were widened and lengthened. The Army Air Corps 14th Antisubmarine Patrol Squadron utilized the field through 1943, and, thereafter, fell under the navy for the duration of World War II. (MANGHA.)

Carl Allen showcases the insignia of the Massachusetts Air National Guard, designed by noted artist Paul F. Seavey in 1924. The blue field once stood for the waters of Boston Harbor, and today for the skies above Massachusetts and the Atlantic Ocean surrounding Cape Cod. The gold ring represents unity, the gull vigilance and keen vision. (MANGHA.)

Airdrome officers were appointed to act as the base commander's representative, the post's officer of the day. This image was taken in October or November 1941, when the 26th Infantry Division headed south for maneuvers. The airdrome officer sits outside the operations tent at Knollwood Airport, Southern Pines, North Carolina. (MANGHA.)

Following the end of the World War II, several changes occurred that altered the military aviation story at Camp Edwards. First in 1946, the base was deactivated and placed on caretaker status. Also in that year, the runway was lengthened to 8,000 feet, a product of the ever-growing size of American military aircraft. Then in 1947, the Army Air Corps broke away from the U.S. Army to become the U.S. Air Force. The 101st Observation Squadron was reactivated that year, and the relationship between the U.S. Air Force and the National Guard was solidified. The players were all the same, just bearing different names. Different names meant it was time for new signs, like this one at the entrance to the base. In 1948, the name changed officially to Otis Air Force Base. (MANGHA.)

The skies certainly looked different over Cape Cod once the 551st Airborne Early Warning and Control Wing arrived at Otis in 1954. The following year, the unit received its first aircraft, an RC-121D, eventually upgrading to the EC-121H Warning Star in 1963. Not all was ready for the arrival of the Warning Stars. Without hangars long enough to accommodate the entirety of the planes—113 feet—the 551st was forced to retrofit doors to close around the tail sections of the craft, leaving them exposed to the elements. (MANGHA.)

NEW+C AIRCRAST PARKING RAMP
FIELD MAINT. SQDN. HANGAR

According to the history of the 102nd Fighter Wing, "Until 1973, Otis was the largest Aerospace Defense Command base in the world and the only Air Force base named for a doctor." (MNG.)

The cold war years saw heavy usage of the Otis Air Force Base. Apart from the various squadrons of the 551st, the following units flew out of the installation: 33rd Tactical Fighter Wing, 1948–1957; 60th Fighter-Interceptor Squadron, 1948–1950 and 1955–1971; 59th Fighter-Interceptor Squadron, 1948–1952; 58th Fighter-Interceptor Squadron, 1948–1959; 50th Fighter-Interceptor Wing, 1949–1951; 81st Fighter Squadron, 1949–1951; 437th Fighter-Interceptor Squadron, 1952–1955; 119th Aircraft Control and Warning Squadron, 1952–1953; 19th Air Refueling Squadron, 1960–1966; 553rd Reconnaissance Wing, 1967; and 1st Special Operations Wing, 1969–1972. (MANGHA.)

As stated earlier in the book, social recreation away from the rigors of military training went a long way to keep morale high during tense times. Formal dances held on base, or even just taking to the dance floor informally once the music started, offered a chance to blow off steam. Sometimes a newspaper and a cold beer could do the trick as well. (MANGHA.)

Fourth of July celebrations offered the chance for one and all to let their guards down—so to speak, as round-the-clock flights still continued—and mingle on a closer man-to-man basis than the rigid military ranking system usually allowed. Photographers were sure to catch as much of the action as they could for base newsletters. (MANGHA.)

As shown in this July 1957 image, dress uniforms came out for invited guests, with white gloves and snappy salutes all around. (MANGHA.)

Basic military training of air force recruits in the 1950s became a subject of national attention with severe overcrowding of Lackland Air Force Base in Texas. Sen. Lyndon B. Johnson sent a subcommittee to investigate the situation and was told that 19,000 men were sleeping in tents at the base, for which they remonstrated the air force. To streamline the process, basic training was shortened from 13 to 8 weeks and new training centers opened, including one at Sampson Air Force Base in upstate New York. The skills learned in basic training elsewhere were honed in drills and marches at duty stations, as shown here at Otis in 1955. (MANGHA.)

Cold war tensions reached their heights in the early 1960s with the Cuban Missile Crisis, the U-2 incident, and the Berlin Crisis. As the Soviets threatened to close West Berlin to the west, Pres. John F. Kennedy called for an escalation in troop strength and an increase in military spending. By October, the Air National Guard's 102nd Tactical Fighter Wing was recalled and prepared to go overseas. Arch Bishop Richard Cardinal Cushing distributed communion to airmen just before their departure to Phalsbourg, France, in late 1961. (MANGHA.)

With 82 F-86 Sabres, the 102nd crossed the Atlantic with a mission of close air support for NATO ground forces, should any military action arise, as well as interdiction of enemy aircraft. The men of the 102nd participated in joint exercises with foreign troops, but political tensions eased enough that the unit was called home on May 7, 1962. Brig. Gen. Charles W. Sweeney, far right with the hat, led the 102nd there and back. (MANGHA.)

General Sweeney was a story himself. Born in Lowell on December 27, 1919, he learned to fly in Quincy while in high school, joining the U.S. Army in 1941 as an air cadet. He spent the war in preparation for its last offensive. As commander of the 393rd Bombardment Squadron, in July 1945, he flew test flights to ready himself for the first bomb he would drop on the enemy after four years in service. On August 9, 1945, he commanded *Bockscar*, a B-29 Superfortress, headed for the Japanese city of Kokura, but weather diverted the flight, sending the plane in search of a secondary target. Over Nagasaki, Bockscar dropped "Fat Man," a plutonium bomb that killed at least 70,000 Japanese and led to the end of World War II six days later. From 1955 to 1976, General Sweeney commanded the Massachusetts Air National Guard's 102nd Tactical Fighter Wing. (MANGHA.)

In 1973, the air force deactivated Otis Air Force Base, meaning only that the national units left the base and that the task of 24-hour-a-day surveillance fell to the 102nd Fighter Wing of the Massachusetts Air National Guard. The Massachusetts Army National Guard took command of the rest of Camp Edwards, with the Coast Guard utilizing a portion of the base. The 102nd moved from F-84F Thunderstreaks, to F-100D Supersabres, then F-106 Delta Darts, and later F-15 Eagles, shown here. (MANG.)

Through various interception and training missions and deployments overseas, the F-15s of the 102nd bore the "Minuteman" insignia of the Massachusetts National Guard on the tail and the gull insignia just aft and below the cockpit. In 1999 and 2000, the unit deployed to the Middle East and Europe to take part in Operations Northern Watch and Southern Watch, enforcing no-fly zones around Iraq. (MANG.)

According to Col. Anthony Schiavi, commander of the 102nd Intelligence Wing, on September 11, 2001, Lt. Col. Tim Duffy and Maj. Dan Nash were the first responders to the terrorist attacks on the World Trade Center towers in Manhattan. They arrived just moments after the second strike "and would be the sole ID authority for aircraft, helicopters, etc. that were still airborne after the towers were hit, ensuring that there were no additional threats to the city." For the next six months, flights from the 102nd Fighter Wing flew nonstop patrols as part of Operation Noble Eagle. A closure scare in 2005 threatened the end of the 102nd, but it instead made the transition to an intelligence wing on April 1, 2008, to aid in the war on terror—losing its planes but maintaining its operational status. As of this writing, the Camp Edwards and Otis airbase stories continue. (MANG.)

www.arcadiapublishing.com

Discover books about the town where you grew up, the cities where your friends and families live, the town where your parents met, or even that retirement spot you've been dreaming about. Our Web site provides history lovers with exclusive deals, advanced notification about new titles, e-mail alerts of author events, and much more.

Find Your Place in History.